Perfect Harmony Coloring Books
Dream Garden
Adult Coloring Book

Janet Myrto Richards

Open up a new world of coloring!

The large images in this book allow colorists with hand pain to color easily using markers and very little pressure.

Experienced colorists will be inspired to take it to the next level by microcoloring with extra fine markers and gel pens.

For best results, remove a page from the book and place it on a piece of card stock. The card stock will absorb any ink bleeding through and it makes a great place to test your colors before committing them to the page. You will also have the freedom to turn the page around as you work.

Dream Garden has 30 pages to color!

I hope you enjoy this coloring book.
Please let me know at:

janetmyrtorichards.wordpress.com

I0493523

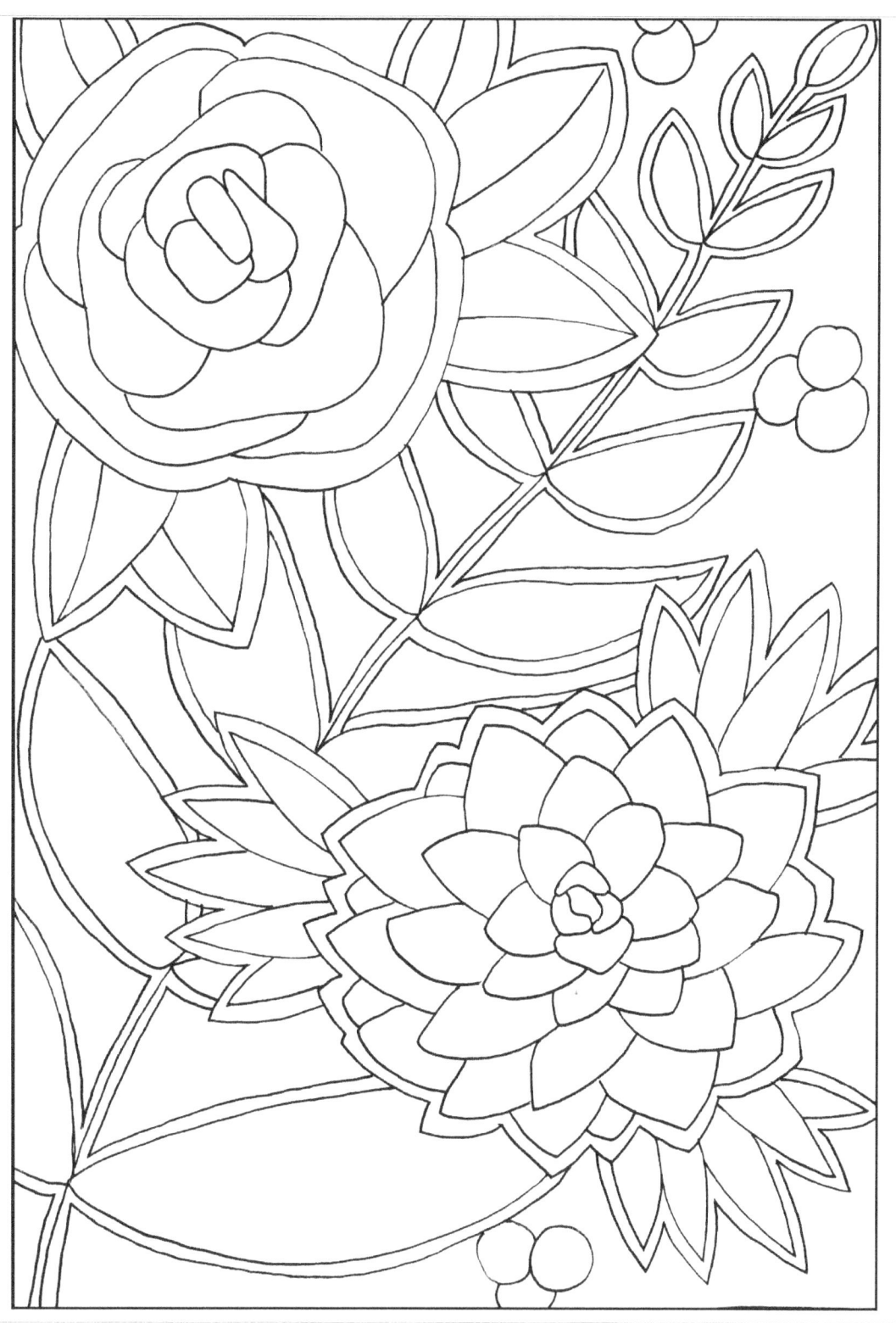

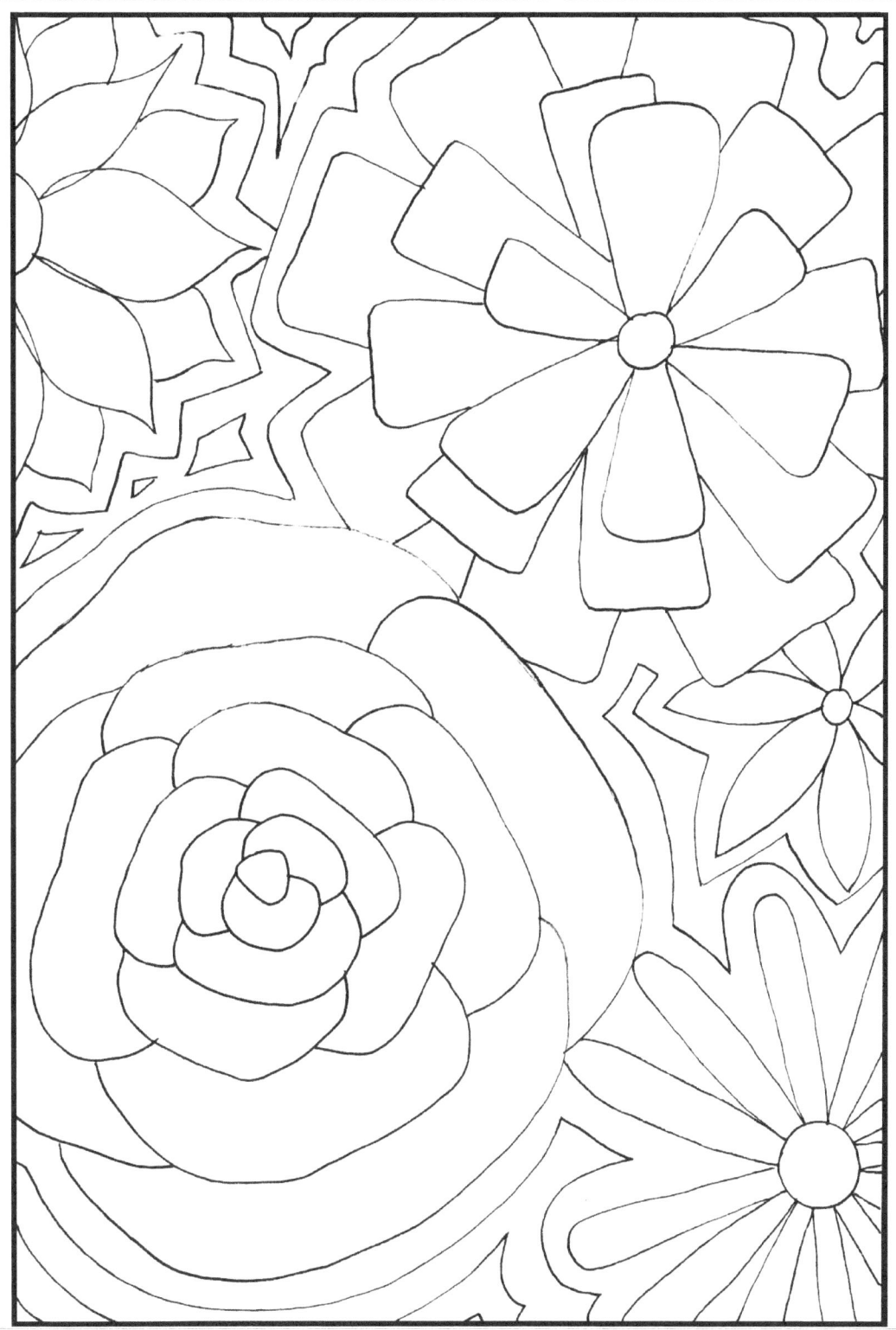

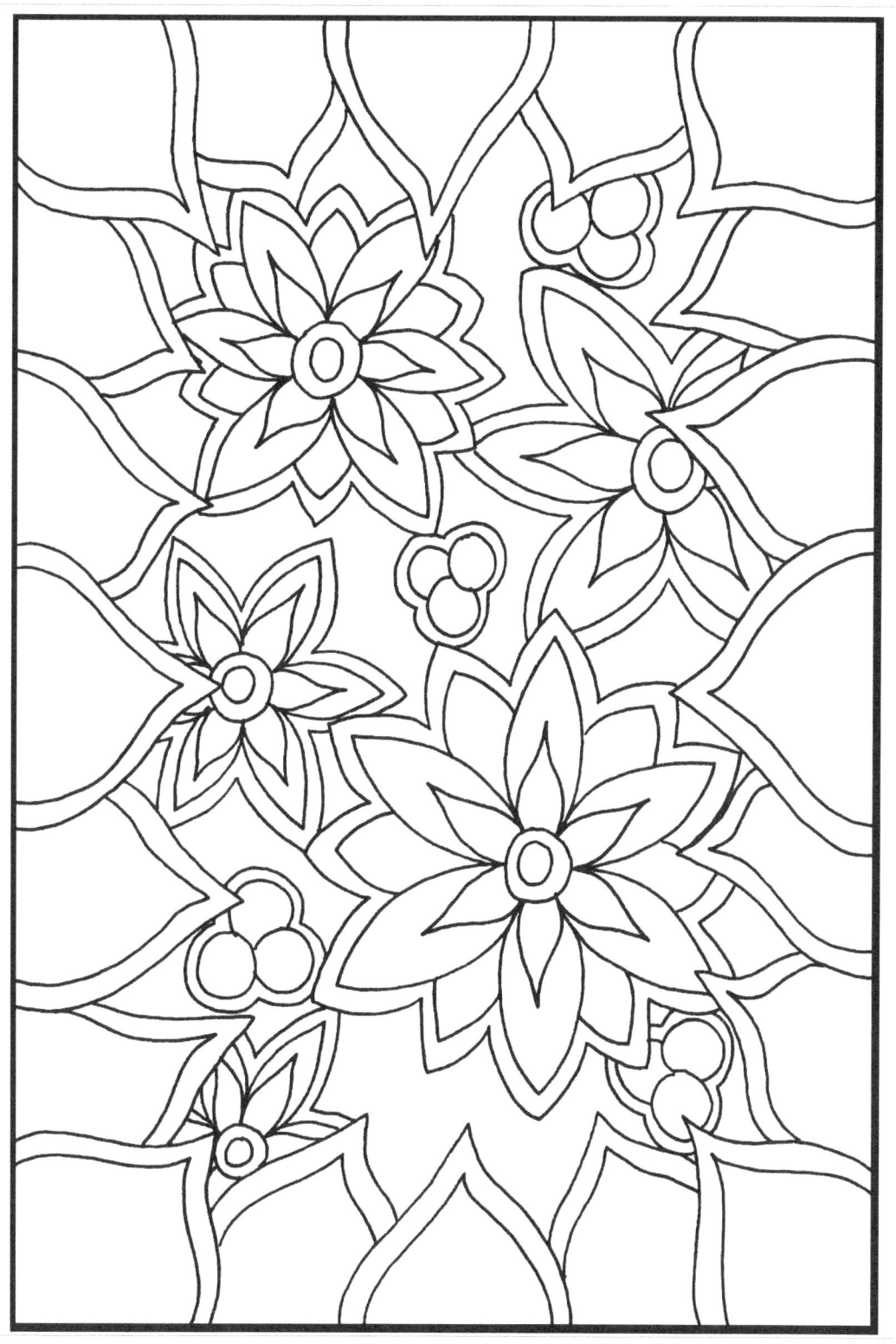

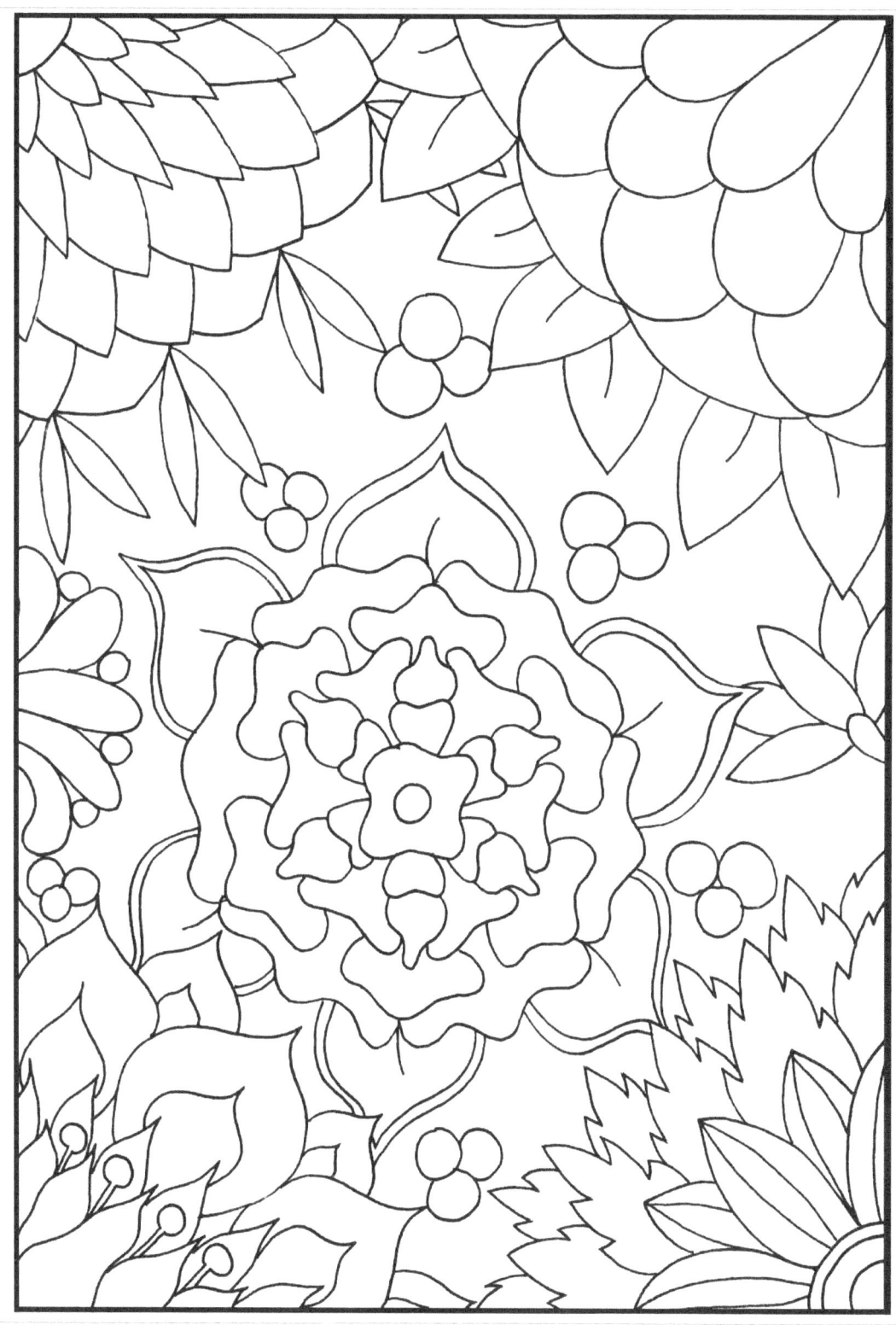

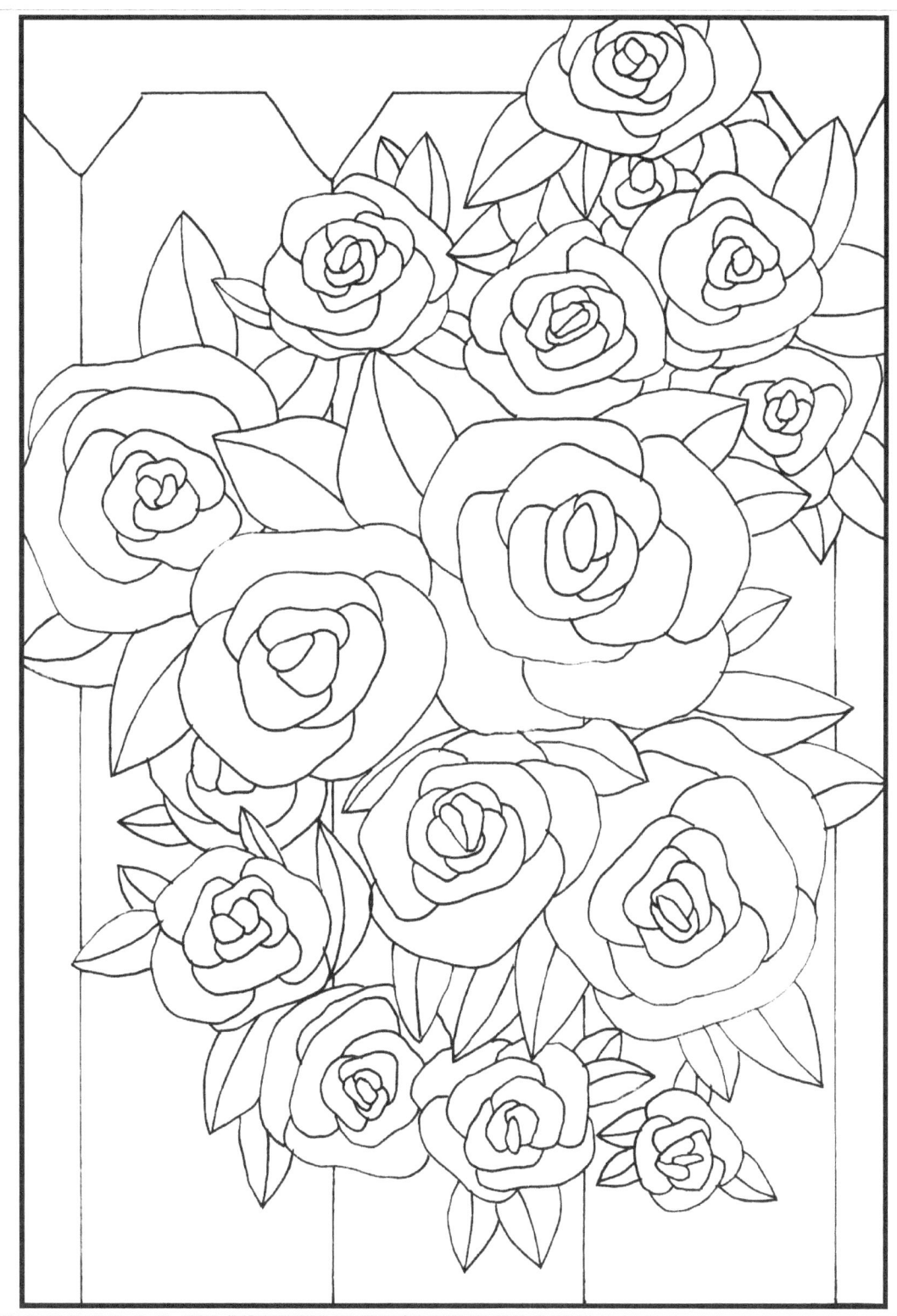

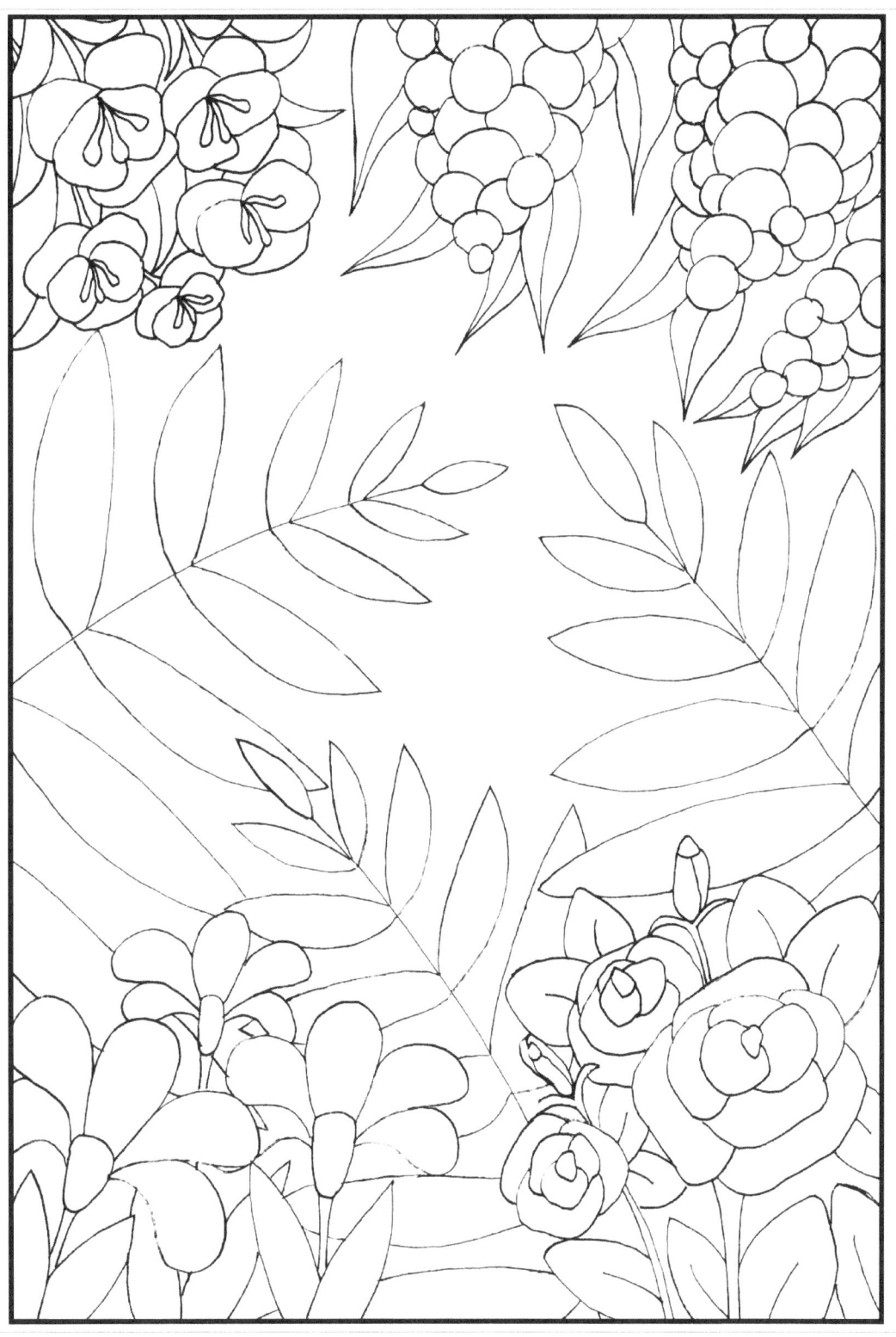

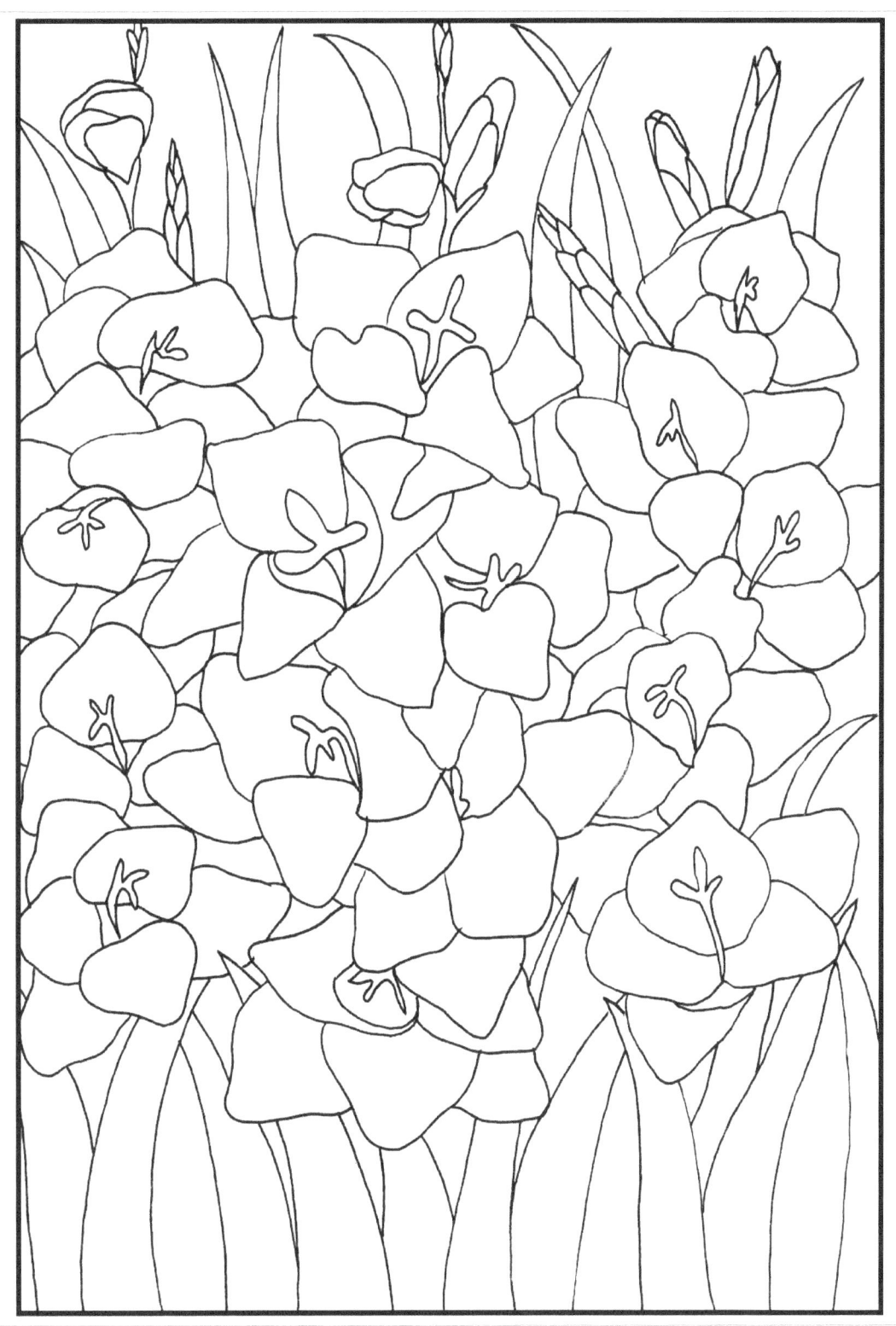

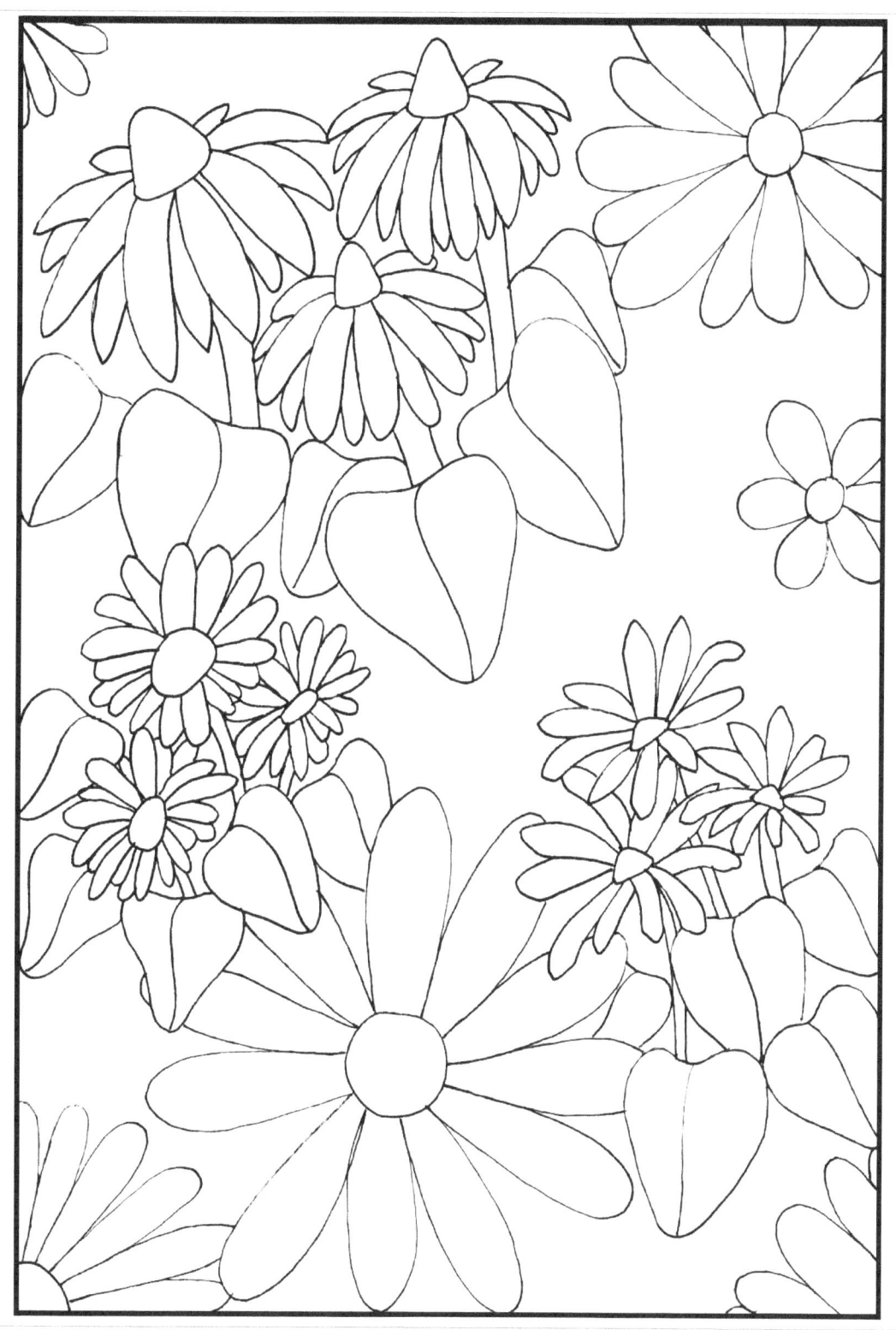

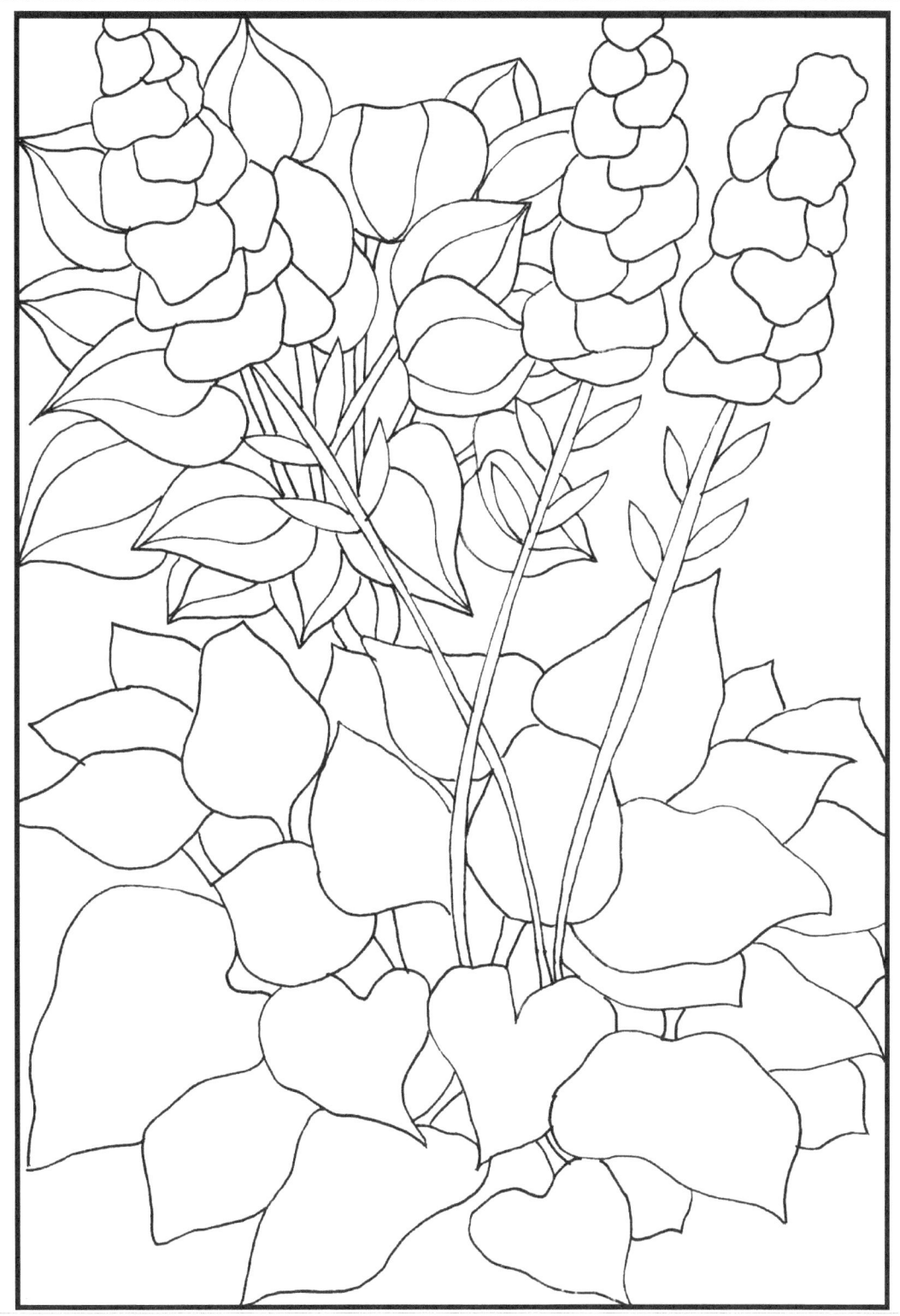

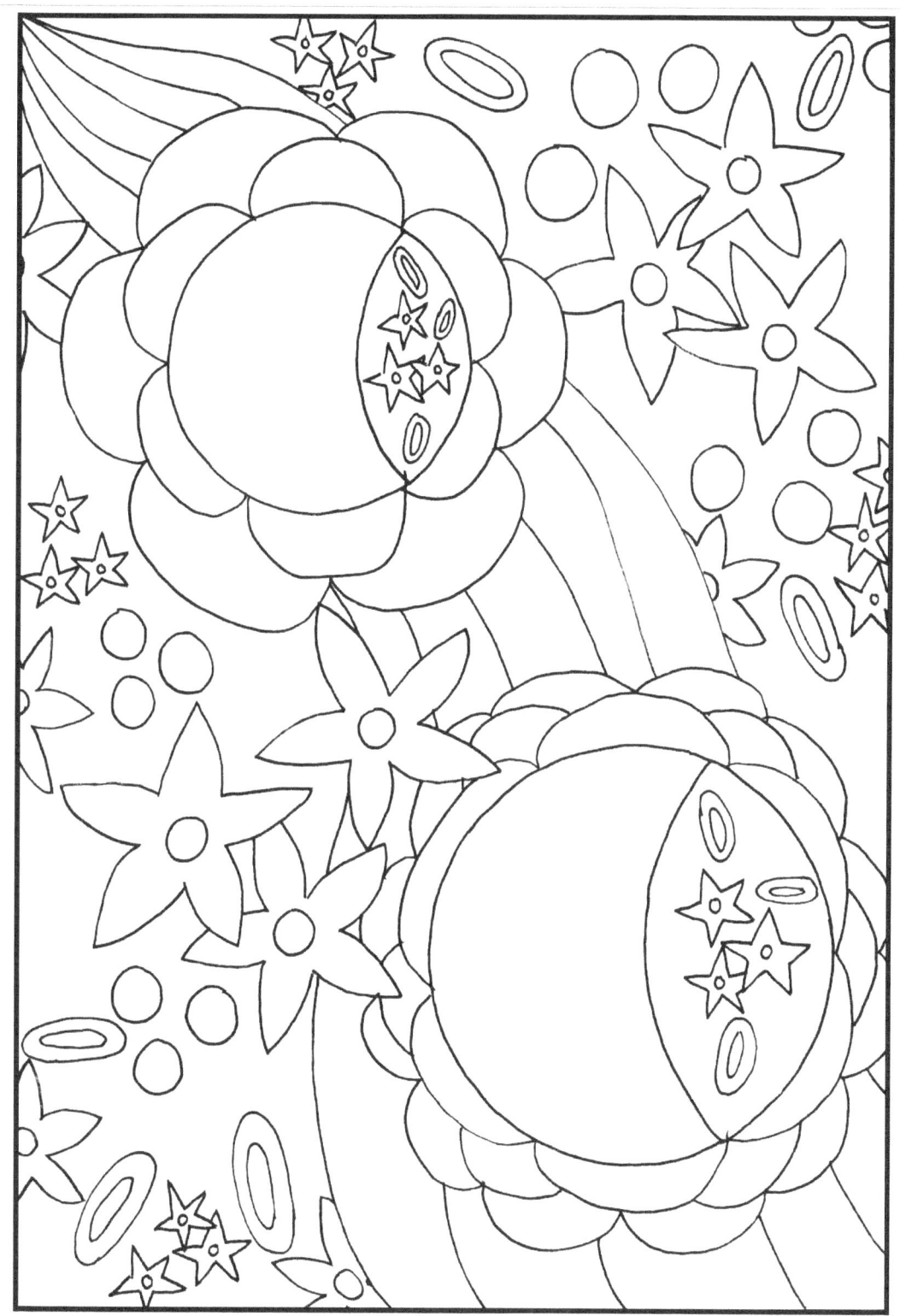

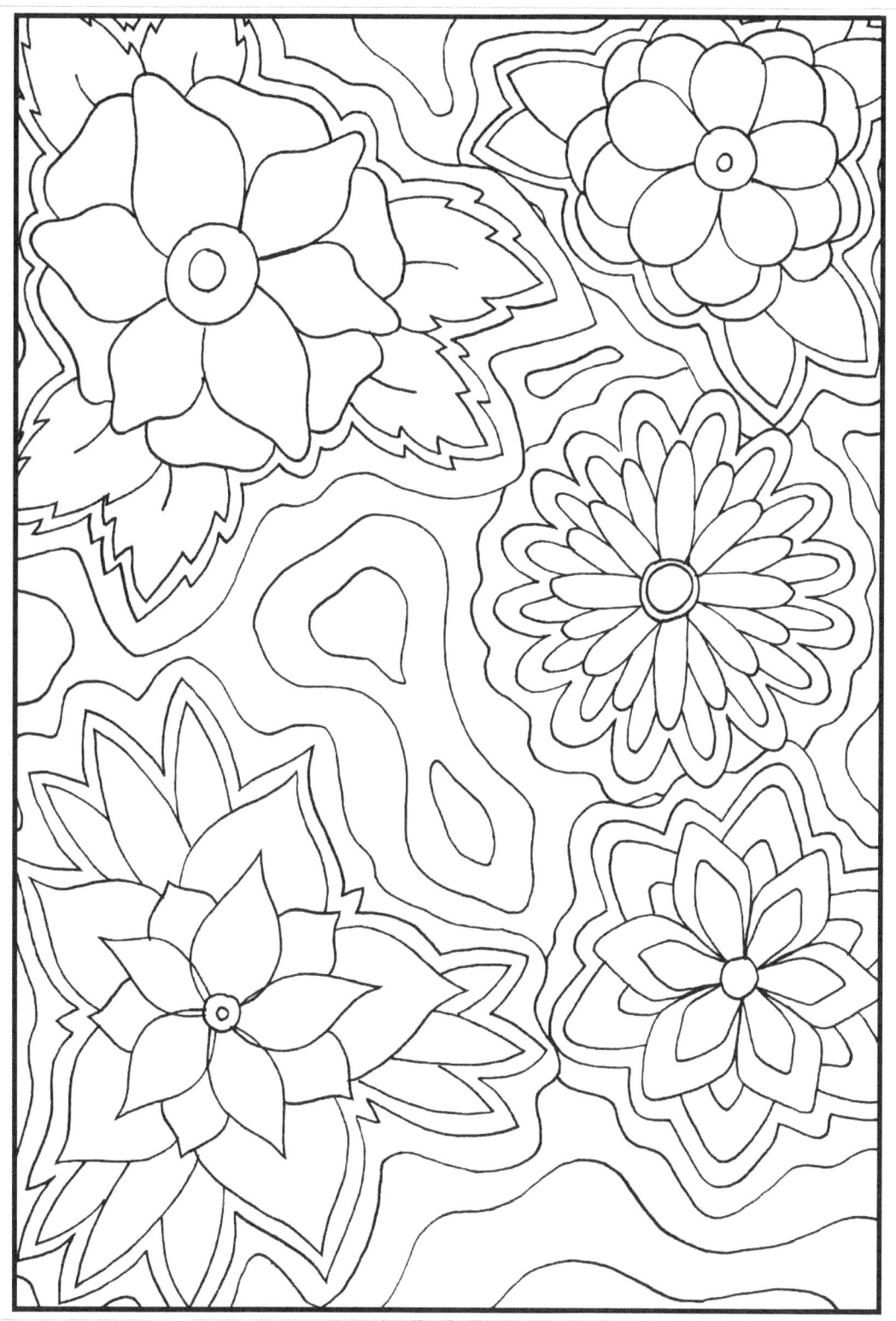

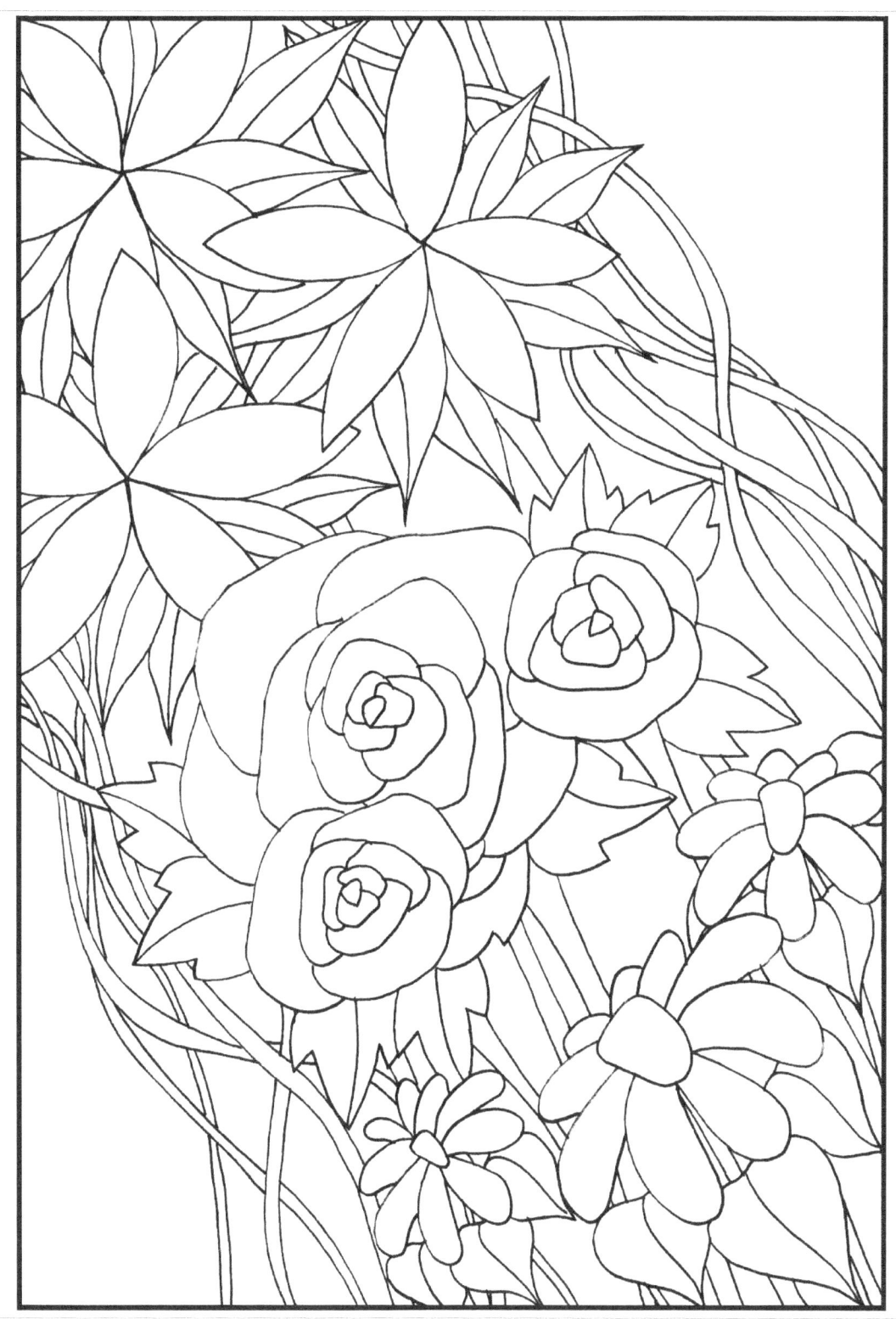

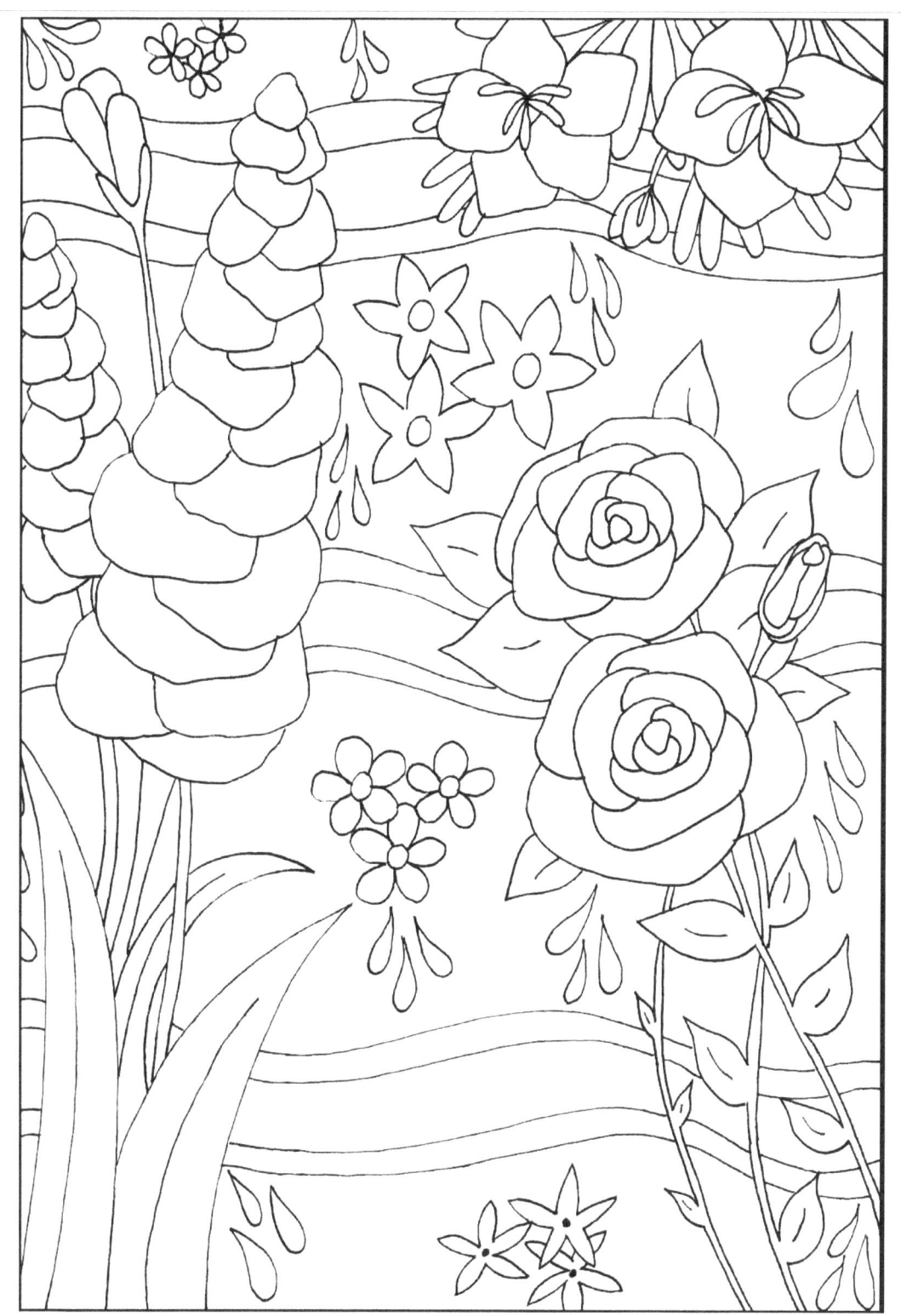

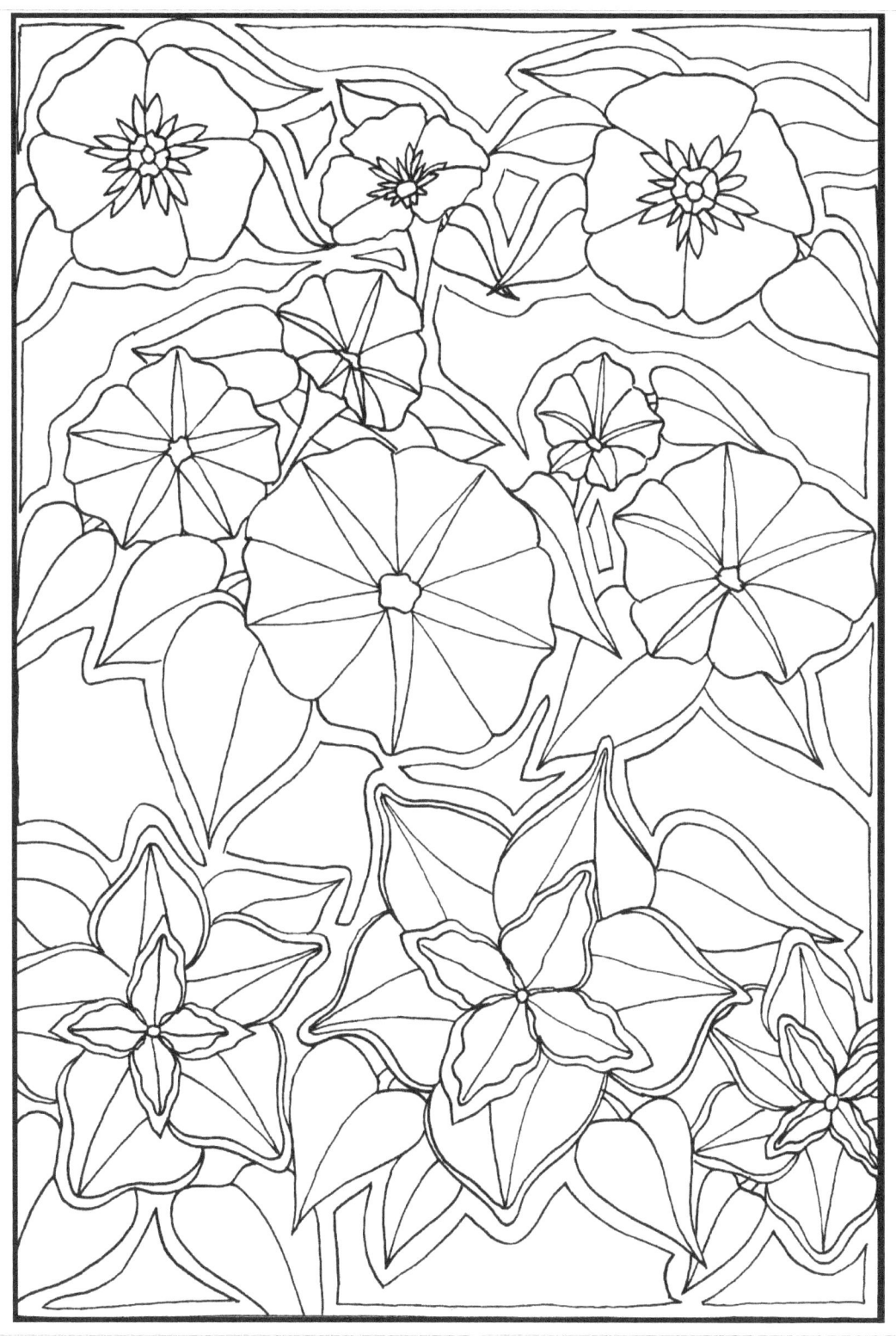

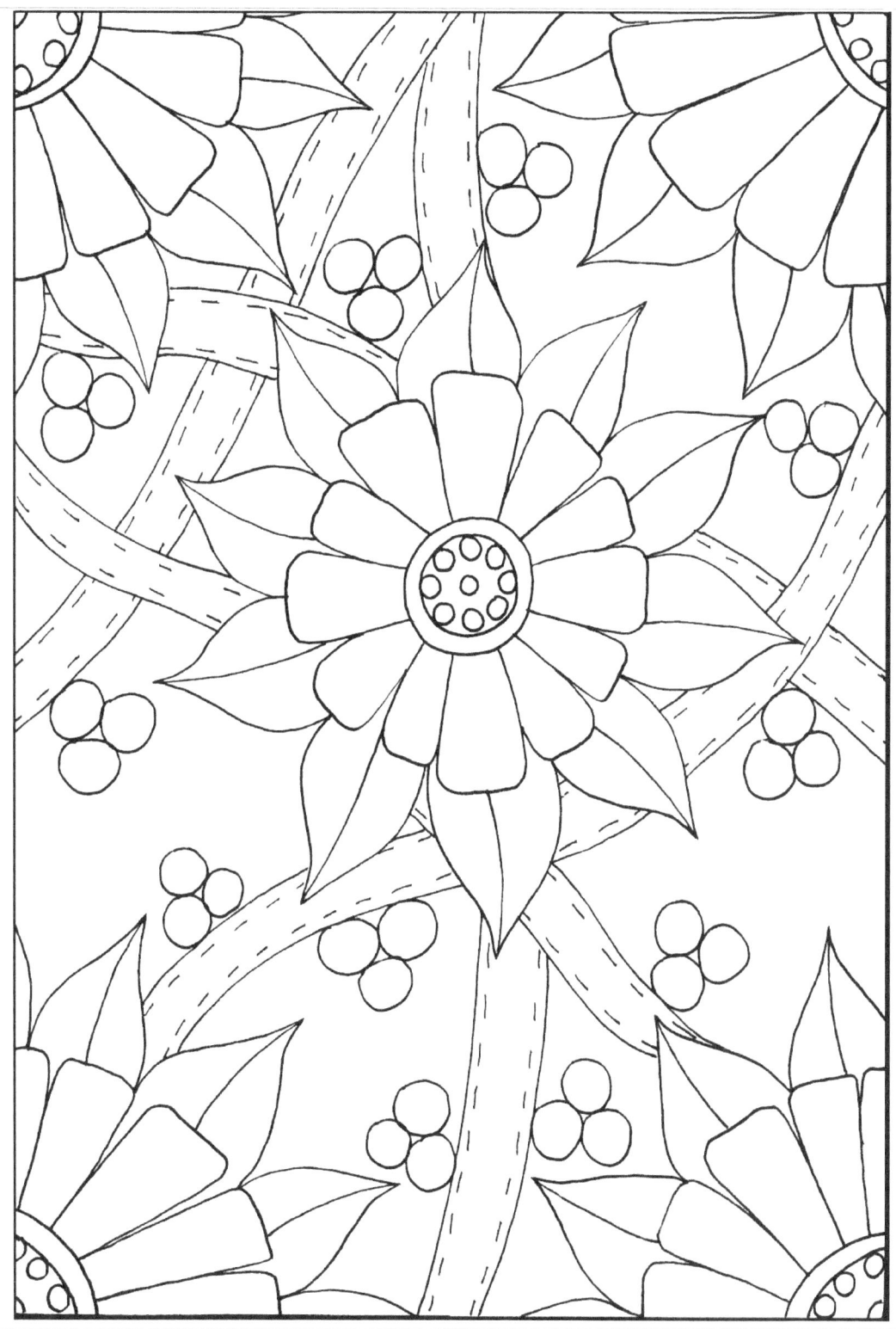

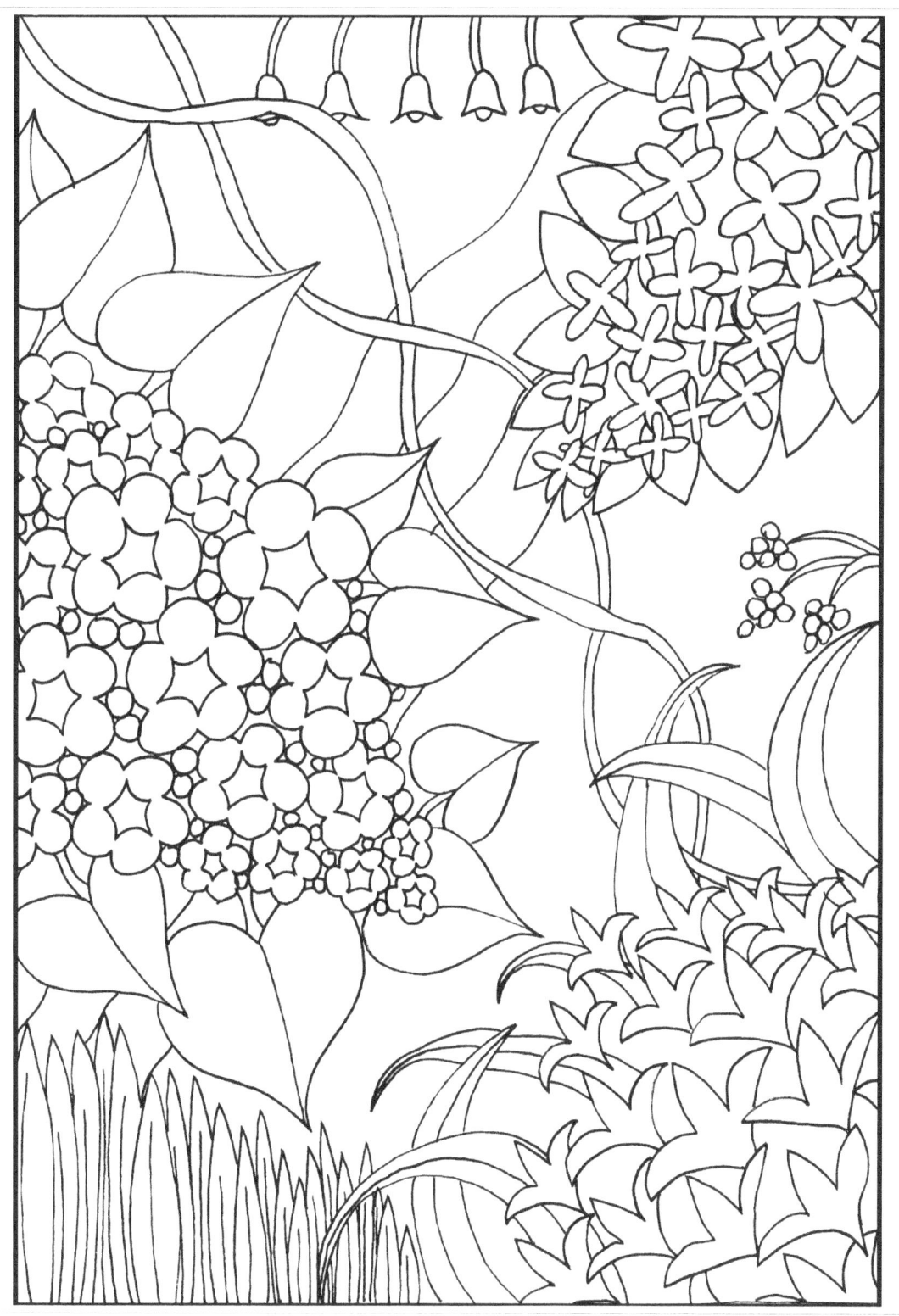

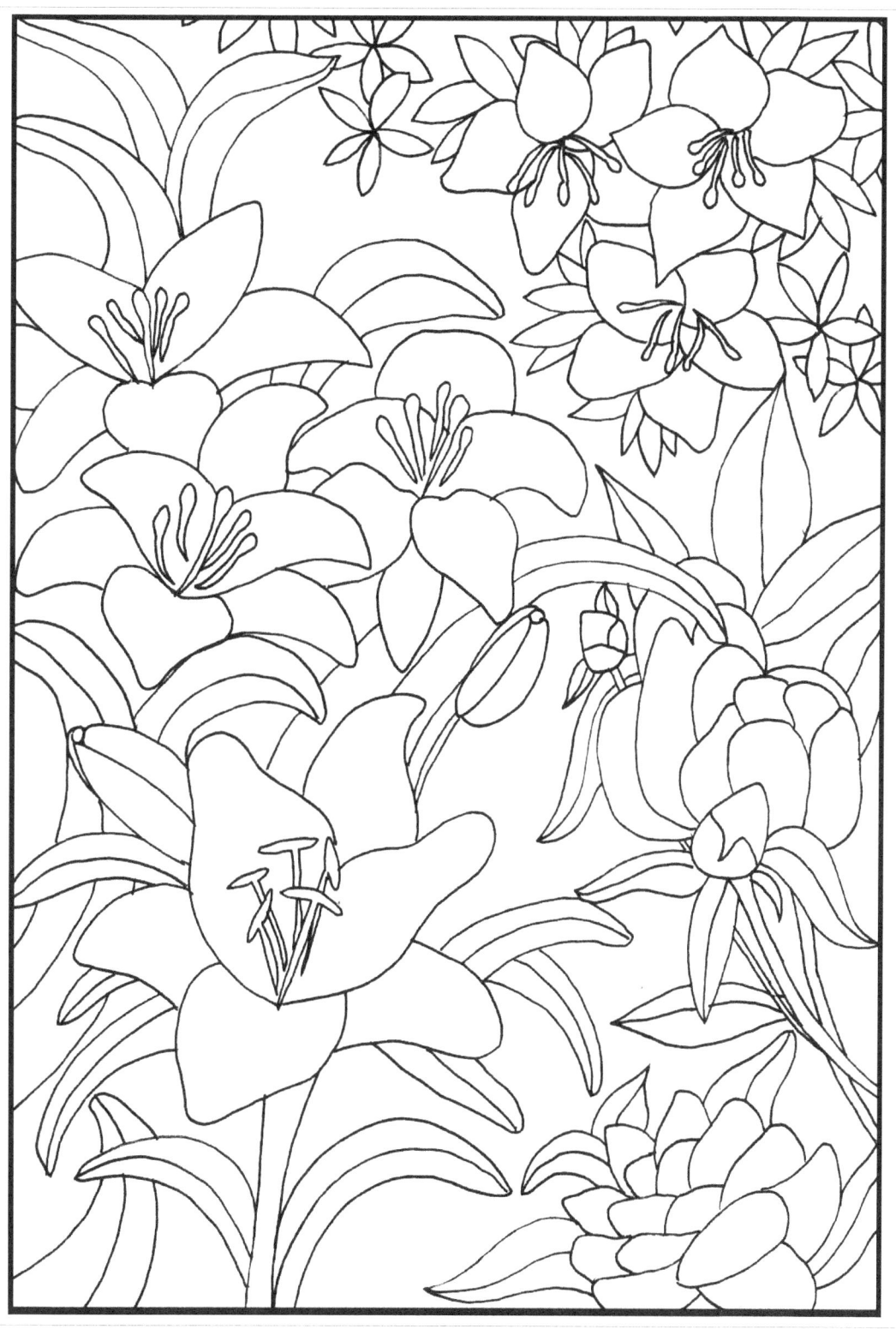

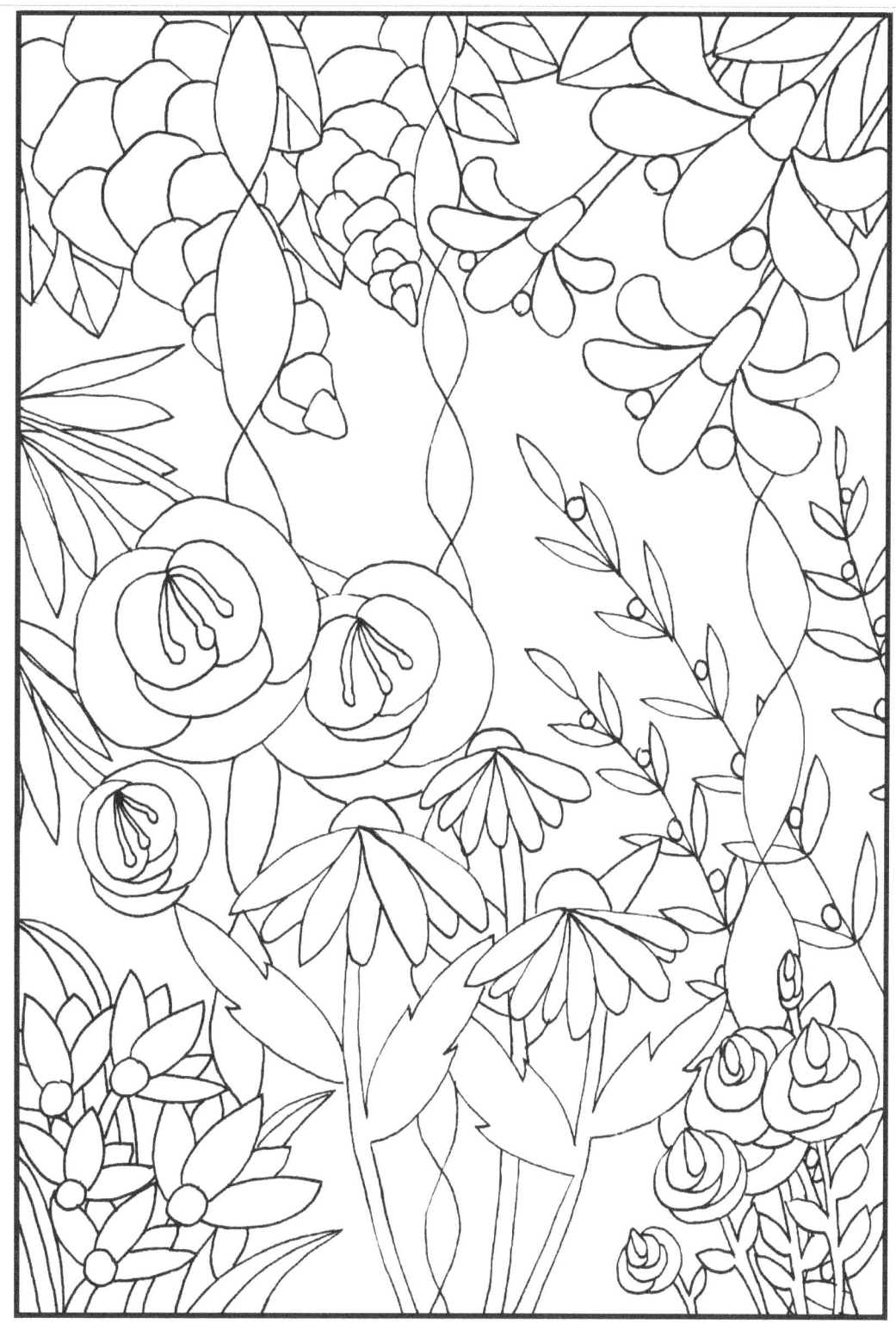

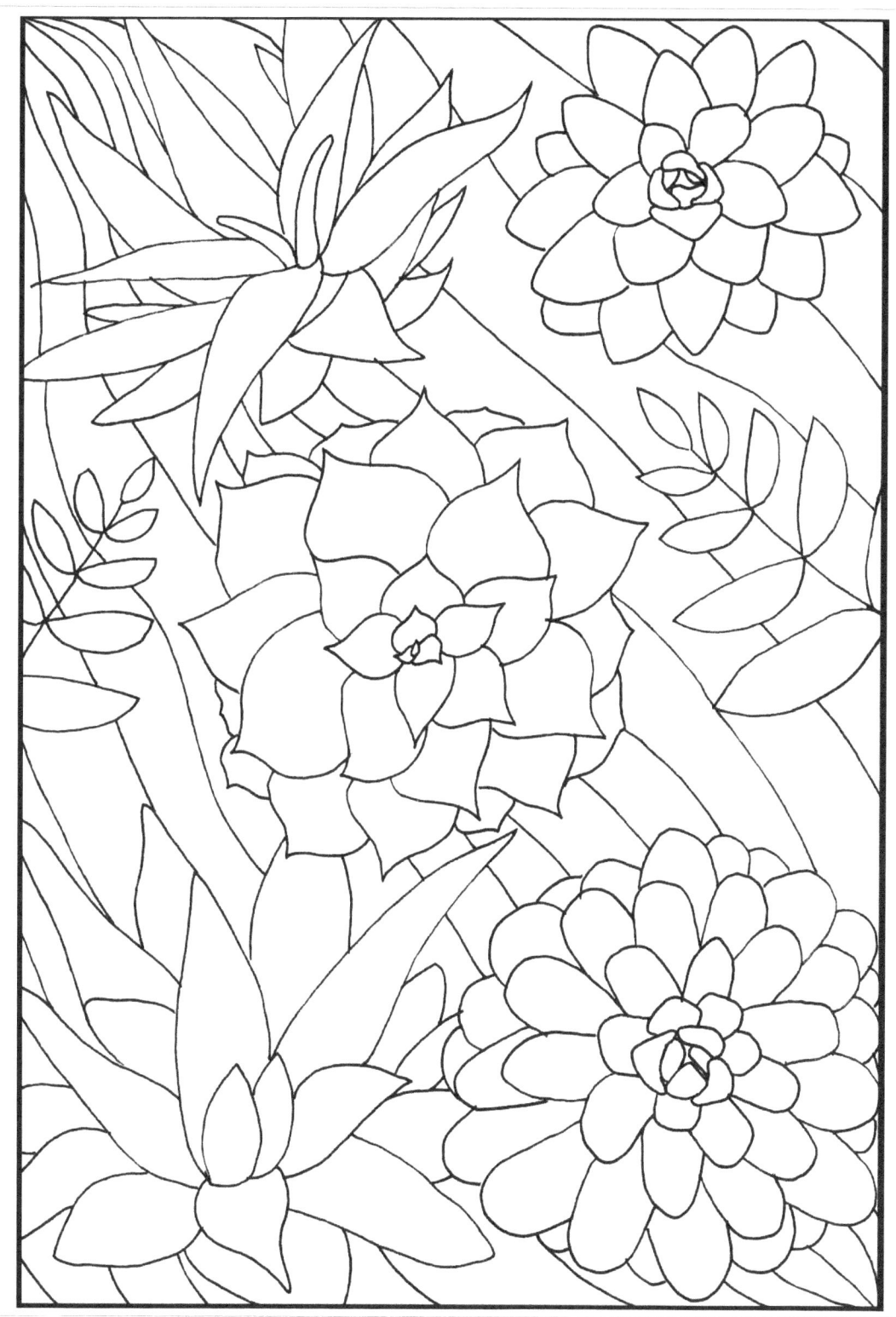

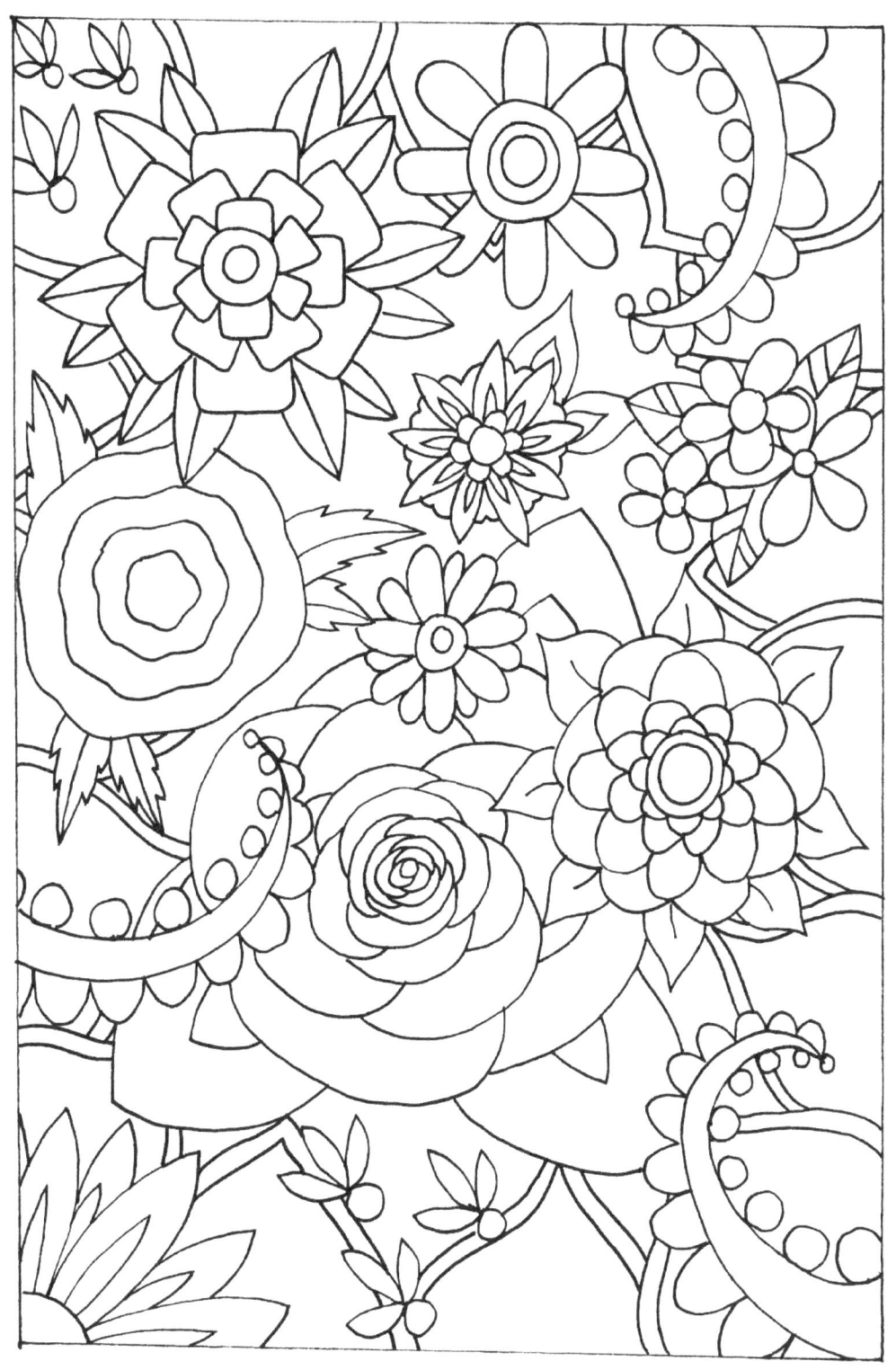

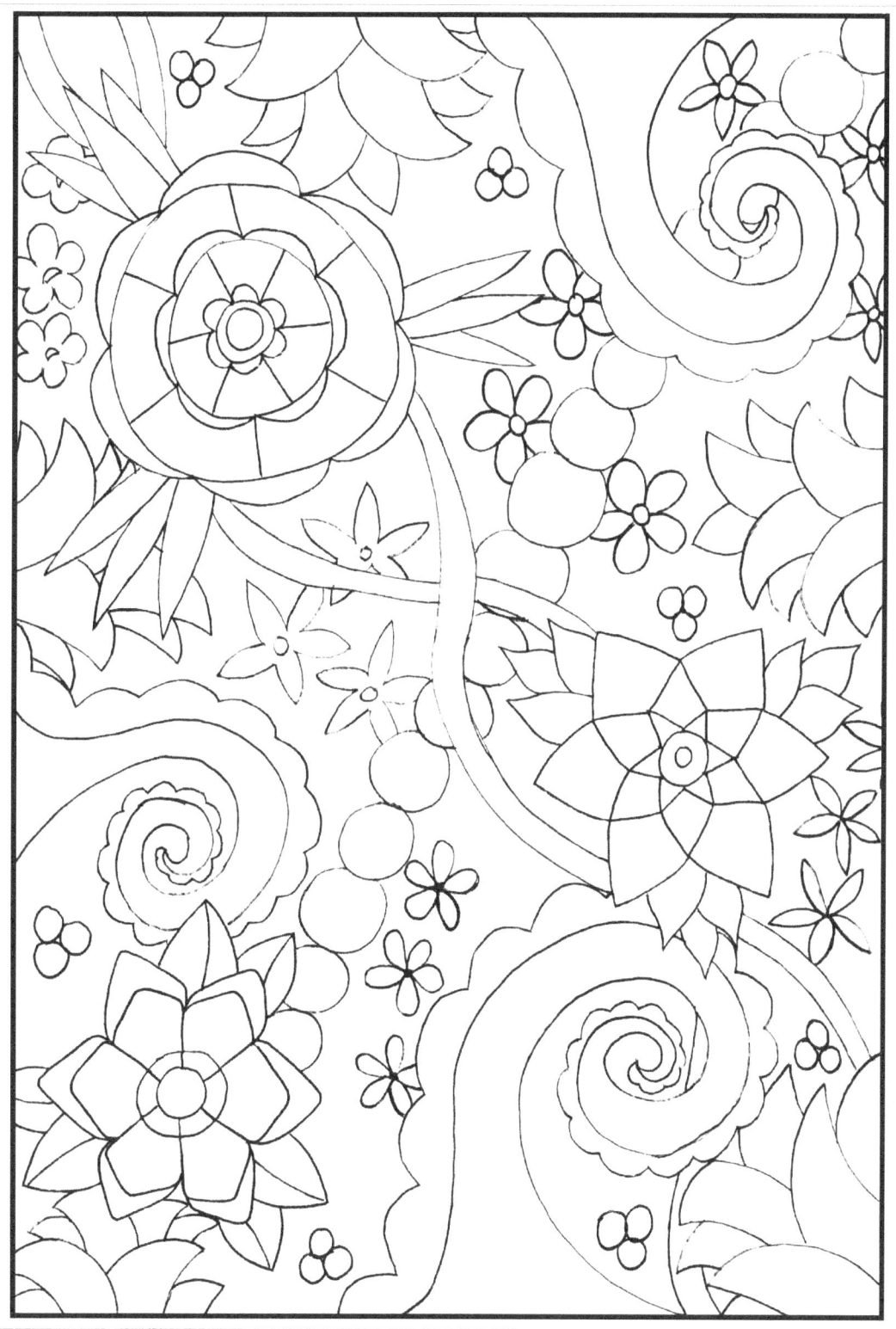

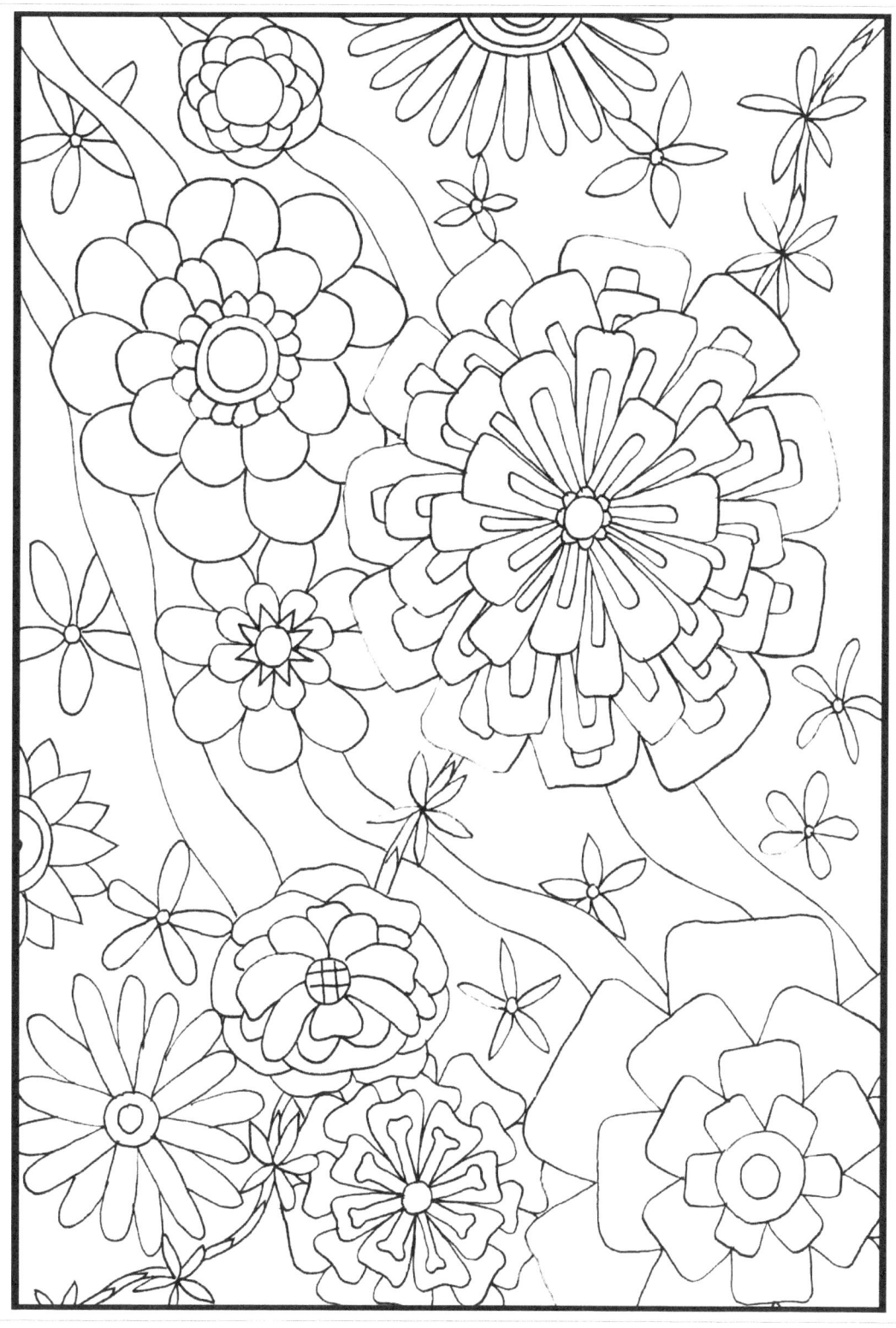

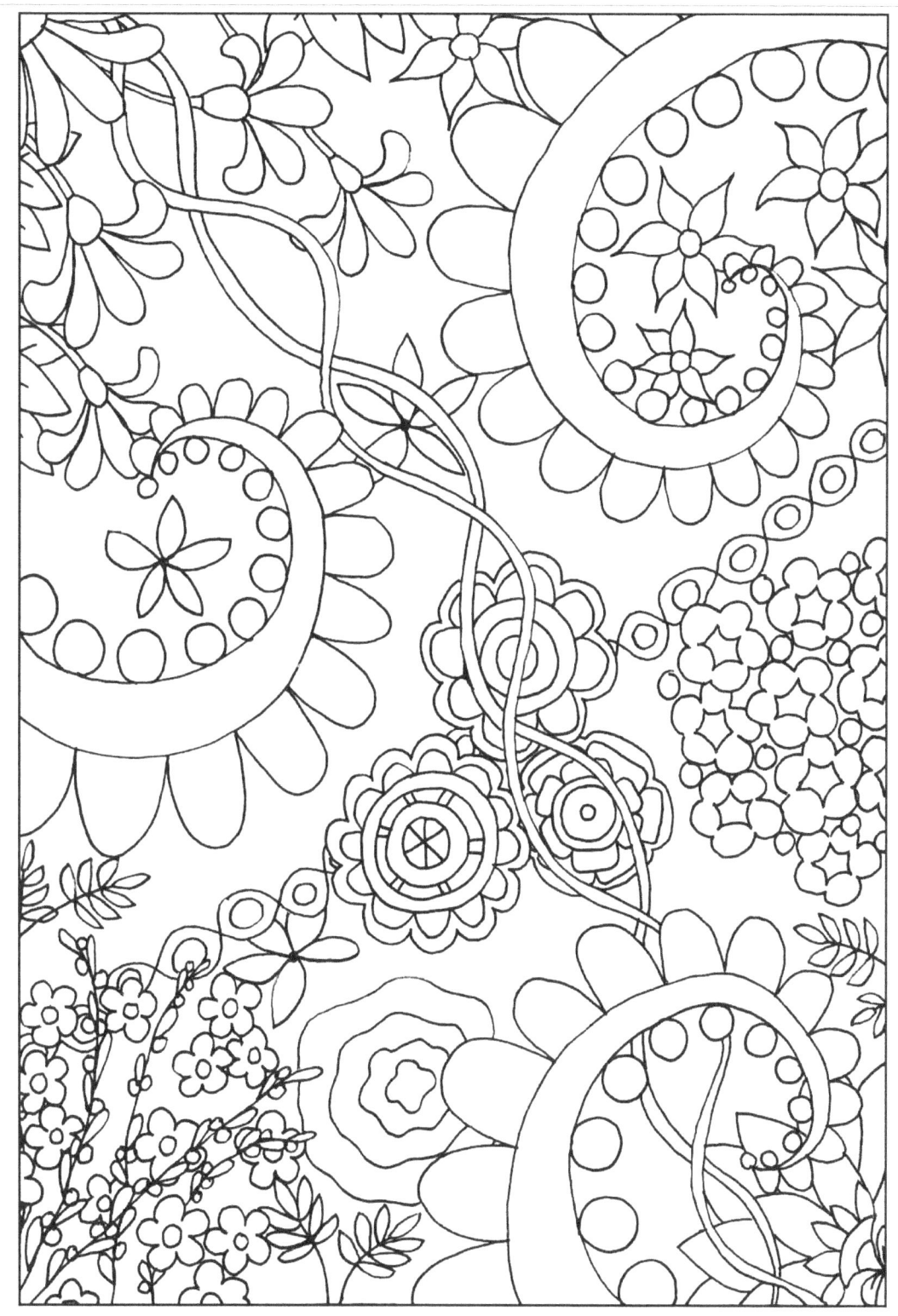

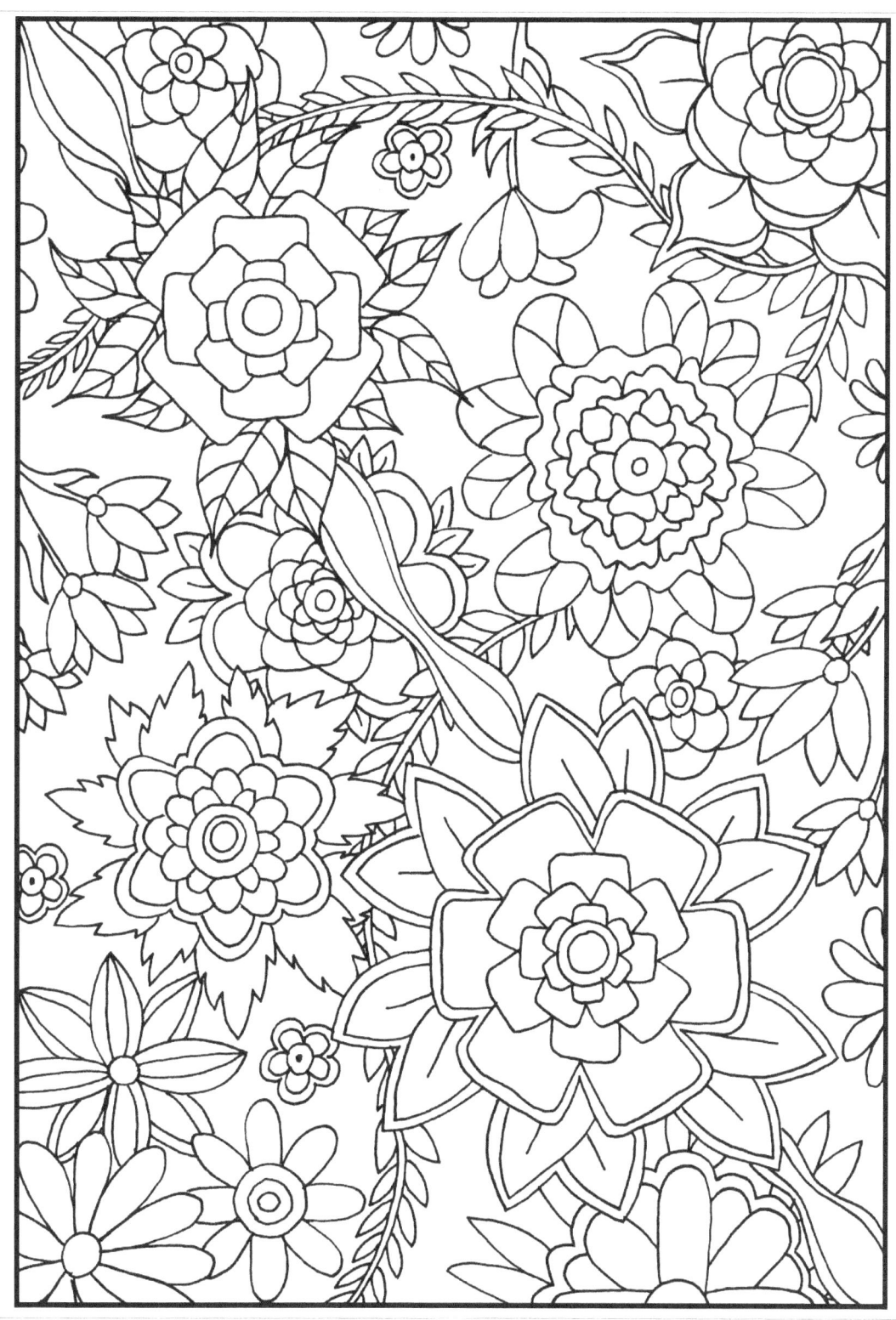

www.ingramcontent.com/pod-product-compliance
Lightning Source LLC
Chambersburg PA
CBHW080543190526
45169CB00007B/2615